URSUS WEHRLI · TIDYING UP ART

# TIDYING UP ART

URSUS WEHRLI

WITH AN INTRODUCTION BY
ALBRECHT GÖTZ VON OLENHUSEN

PRESTEL
MUNICH · BERLIN · LONDON · NEW YORK

A neat thank you to my parents, Brigitta Schrepfer and Nadja Sieger

Front cover: Vincent van Gogh, 1888, *Bedroom at Arles*; Ursus Wehrli, 2002
Back cover: René Magritte, 1953, *Golconde* (detail); Ursus Wehrli, 2002

The Library of Congress Cataloguing-in-Publication data is available;
British Library Cataloguing-in-Publication Data: a catalogue record for this book is available
from the British Library;
Deutsche Bibliothek holds a record of this publication in the Deutsche Nationalbibliografie;
detailed bibliographical data can be found under: http://dnb.ddb.de

© Prestel Verlag, Munich · Berlin · London · New York 2003
First published in German under the title *Kunst aufräumen*. © 2002 Kein & Aber AG Zurich, Switzerland

Prestel books are available worldwide. Please contact your nearest bookseller or one of
the following Prestel offices for information concerning your local distributor:

Prestel Verlag
Königinstrasse 9, 80539 Munich
Tel. +49 (89) 38 17 09-0; Fax +49 (89) 38 17 09-35

Prestel Publishing Ltd.
4 Bloomsbury Place, London WC1A 2QA
Tel. +44 (020) 7323-5004; Fax +44 (020) 7636-8004

Prestel Publishing
175 Fifth Avenue, Suite 402, New York, NY 10010
Tel. +1 (212) 995-2720; Fax +1 (212) 995-2733

www.prestel.com

Translated from the German by Rosie Jackson, Munich
Edited by Christopher Wynne
Designed and typeset by Nick Ditzler
Cover design by Buttgereit und Heidenreich, Haltern
Assisted by Caroline Schubiger
Originations by Litax AG, Aesch
Production by Proost, Turnhout, Belgium
Printed in Belgium on acid-free paper

ISBN 3-7913-3003-9

# A PLEA FOR TIDY ART

The Swiss *Kunst-Raum & Form* designer, Ursus Wehrli (Dipl. rer. art) from Zurich, has created a radically new process of viewing art. This invention arose from his experience that works of art centring on important, serious or deep themes are capable of exerting an extremely unpleasant effect if not produced, presented and utilized in accordance with certain standards. Patent number 410566 (2002) at the official patent office for intellectual property in Bern assures legal protection for a process which – with the assistance of natural or contrived means – orders art into that state of peaceful repose which achieves a natural, divine order. This involves using original or altered segments from the piece of art, sorting them according to colour, shape, surface or other criteria which may arise, and rearranging them individually or in combination with similar or contrasting pieces. As a result, our vision is emancipated from the normal expectation of seeing combinations of familiar straight lines or flat surfaces, and this specific rearrangement of a wealth of different shapes achieves the sort of new reality which answers the needs of contemporary artistic expression.

This method of processing art – whether old, new or not yet produced – fulfils Swiss and European patenting requirements in that it marks a new stage along the never-ending road of progress, both as a technical innovation and in its capacity to endow the human psyche with a considerably more pleasant aesthetic and moral experience.

Influenced, it seems, by his knowledge of the philosophy of art and aesthetics, Wehrli joins Hegel in striving towards real authenticity in art, towards simplicity, towards the essence of nature, sprituality and art itself – as opposed to the "chaos created by chance, stunted by the immediacy of the senses and the caprice of conditions, circumstances and characters etc." (G. F. W. Hegel, *Lectures on Aesthetics*, collected works, volumes 13 – 15, 1832ff.).

The works Wehrli presents here – from Bruegel to Matisse and Kandinsky – demonstrate the subtlety of his work and are particularly shocking examples. Even those with only a very remote understanding of art will be able to agree with the philosopher in view of these disorganized art works which make a mockery of mankind's original and ingrained sense of order.

The clear function of this innovation, which has earned the name of *fast art converter* in the international art press, and the immediacy of its effect can be best compared with that of the so-called Bessemer converter: here, the artistic raw material is introduced into in a container made of refined sheet copper, covered with a very secretly prepared acidic lining. It is blown in by pressure (80 – 140 cm mercury compression) via a narrow tube connected to an osmotic pipe at a constant temperature, and within 10 to 15 minutes it is liquefied and converted by means of an artificial "disinfestation".

It was none other than the most famous monologist of modern art, Professor Bazon Brock of Wuppertal, who welcomed the results of experiments converting traditional and contemporary art. He considered them an extremely valuable catalyst causing us to recollect and contemplate original motives, elements and the material itself. As such, this was a move towards the creation of a "Magical New Order of Art": Wehrli replaced the much lamented "loss of centre" (Sedlmaier) with the elementary retrieval of autochthonous means – and thus he confronted an age characterized by radical confusion and deconstruction with a predetermination of a higher order. This is the paradigm of the postmodern age – newly sifted, structured and ordered – which in this way opens a visual path towards a clearly positioned transcendence of art.

Following years of courageous but unsuccessful attempts by the likes of Georges Vatongerloo or Max Bill, who tried to achieve a mathematically influenced rationalisation of art and logical support of human thought  through ordered visual perception of objects, our search for the basic elements in art (graphically illustrated by the very successful rearrangement of Magritte's three still-life apples) becomes much clearer. We no longer concentrate on confusing details. Instead we are confronted with an overall impression which provides quite a different perspective. This, as demonstrated by Paul Klee's building blocks of colour and Picasso's elementary particles, combines sensitive stability with necessary structuring, thus simultaneously producing an intellectual alternative in the sense of a precisely formed, clear logic of artistic semiotics.

Thus, this new structure in art does not actually propel chaos into *this* ordered system, as maintained by critical theorists like Theodor W. Adorno. It is in fact the opposite. A general aesthetic effect is generated which endows spectators of art with the calm feeling that the purpose of art in society is no longer purely to shock or inflict any other negative effects resulting from the applied chaos theory.

*Albrecht Götz von Olenhusen,*
*Barrister at the Oberlandesgericht (Higher Regional Court) and Certified Art Assessor*

Tidying up Klee's *Color table* "*q<sup>u</sup>1*"

Tidying up Kandinsky's *Red Spot II*

H. MATISSE 52

Tidying up Matisse's *Blue Nude IV*

Tidying up Malevich's *The Woodcutter*

13

Tidying up Magritte's *Golconde*

Tidying up Picasso's *Ostrich*

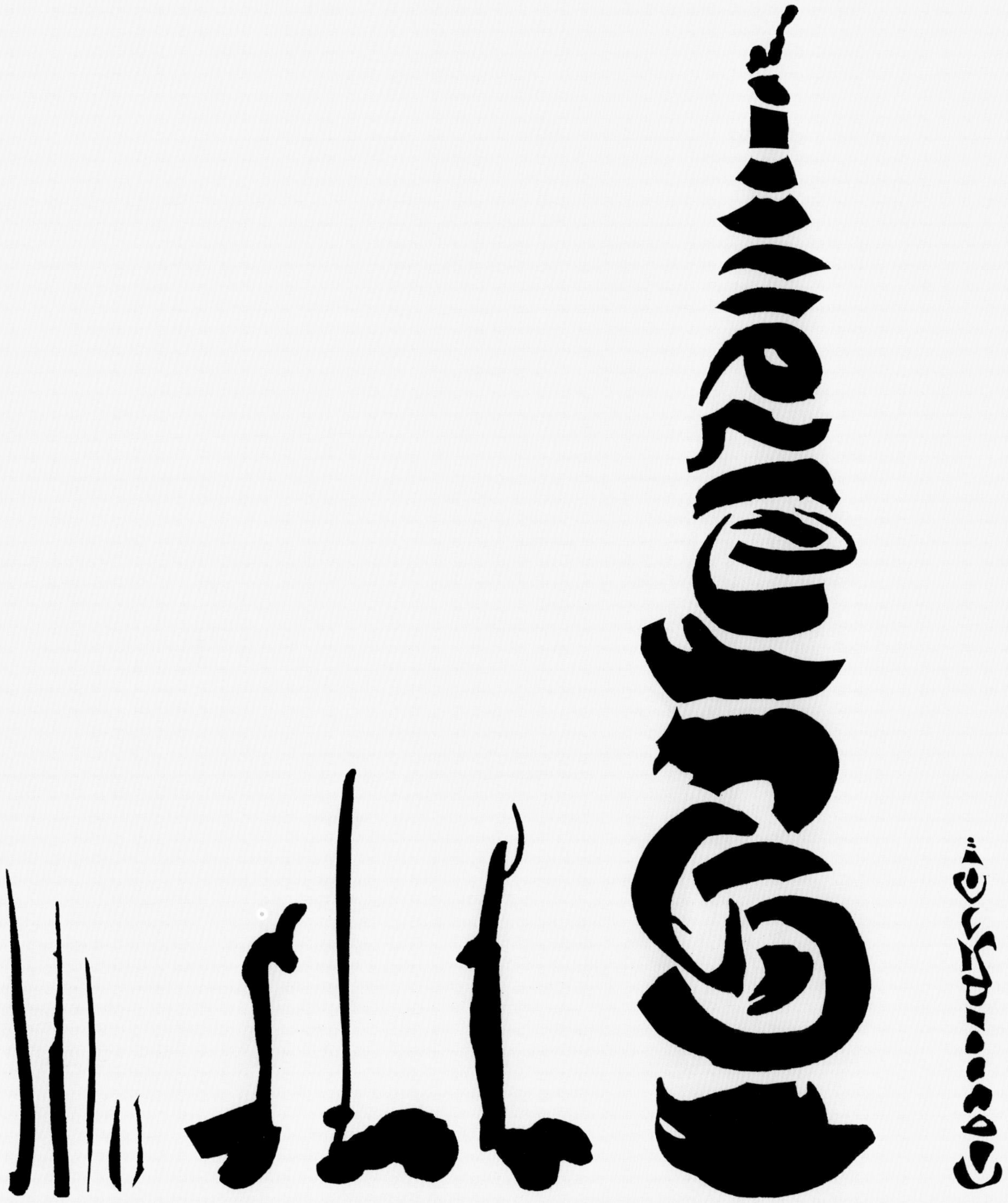

Tidying up Van Gogh's *Bedroom at Arles*

Tidying up Jawlensky's *Mystical Head: Galka*

From Piet's patches to meticulous Mondrian

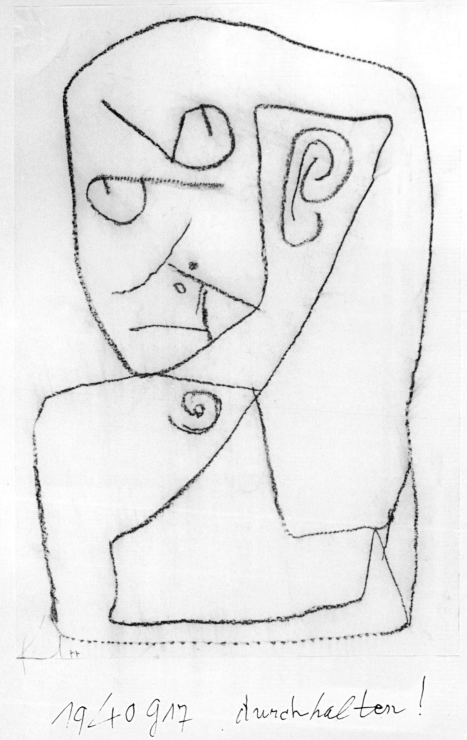

19 40 g 17    durchhalten!

Tidying up Klee's *stick it out!*

Tidying up Seurat's *Models*

Tidying up Malevich's *Suprematism*

Tidying up Picasso's *The Red Armchair*

34

Tidying up Kandinsky's *Sky Blue*

Tidying up Macke's *The Miliner's Shop Window*

Tidying up Lichtenstein's *Grrrrrrrrrr!!*

GRRRRRRRRRRG

· X 5711

41

Tidying up Bruegel's village square

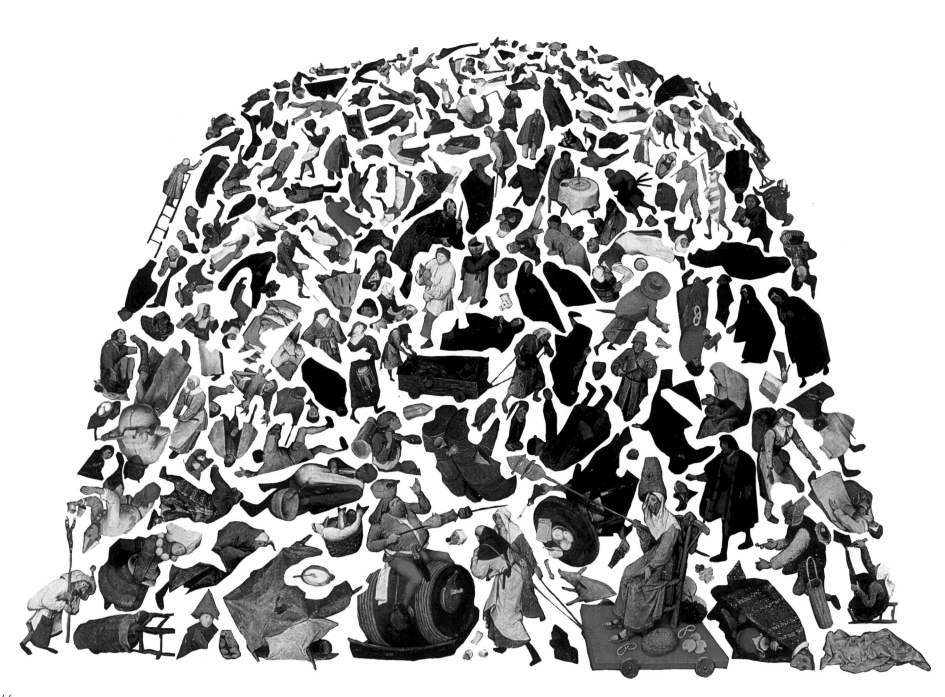

AAAAAAAA aaaaaaaaaaaaaaaaaaaaaaaaaaaaaaaaaaaaa aaaaaaaaaaaaaaaaaaaaaaaaaaaaaaaaaaaaaaaaaaaaa aaaaaaaaaaaaaaaaaaaaaaaaaaaaaaaaaaaaaaaaaaaa aaaaaaaaaaaaaaaaaaaaaaaaaaaaaaaaaaaaaaaaaaaa*aaaaaa*

BBBBBB*B* bbbbbbbbbbbbbbbbbbbbb*bbbbb*

CC cccccccccccccccccccccccccccccccccccccccccc ccccccccccccccccccccccccccccccccccccc*cccc*

D ddddddddddddddddddddddddddddddddddddddddd ddddddddddddddddddddddddddddddddddddddd*dddd*

EE eeeeeeeeeeeeeeeeeeeeeeeeeeeeeeeeeeeeeeeee eeeeeeeeeeeeeeeeeeeeeeeeeeeeeeeeeeeeeeeeeee eeeeeeeeeeeeeeeeeeeeeeeeeeeeeeeeeeeeeeeeeee eeeeeeeeeeeeeeeeeeeeeeeeeeeeeeeeee*eeeeeeeeee*

F*F*F* fffffffffffffffffffffffffffffffff*fffffff*

GGG*G* gggggggggggggggggggggggggggggggg*gggggggg*

HHHH*H* hhhhhhhhhhhhhhhhhhhhhhhhhhhhhhhhh hhhhhhhhhhhhhhhhhhhhhhhhhhhhhhhhhhhhh hhhhhhhhhhhhhhhhhhhhhhhhhhhhhhh*hhhhhhh*

IIIII iiiiiiiiiiiiiiiiiiiiiiiiiiiiiiiiiiiiiiiiiiiiiii iiiiiiiiiiiiiiiiiiiiiiiiiiiiiiiiiiiii*iiiiiiiiiiiiii*

jj

KKK kkkkkkkkkkkkkkk

L lllllllllllllllllllllllllllllllllllllllllllllllllll*llll*

MMMM mmmmmmmmmmmmmmmmmmmmmmmmmmmmm mmmmmmmmmmmmmmmmmmmmmmmmmmmmmmmm*mmmm*

N nnnnnnnnnnnnnnnnnnnnnnnnnnnnnnnnnnnnnn nnnnnnnnnnnnnnnnnnnnnnnnnnnnnnnnnnnnn nnnnnnnnnnnnnnnnnnnnnnnnnnnnnnn*nnnnnnnnnn*

OOO ooooooooooooooooooooooooooooooooooooooo ooooooooooooooooooooooooooooooooooooooooo ooooooooooooooooooooooooooooooooooooooo*ö*

PPPP pppppppppppppppppppppppppppppppppppppppp ppppppppppppppppppppppppppp*pppppppp*

qqq

R*R* rrrrrrrrrrrrrrrrrrrrrrrrrrrrrrrrrrrrrrrrrrr rrrrrrrrrrrrrrrrrrrrrrrrrrrrrrrrrrrrrrrrr*rrrrrrrr*

SSS sssssssssssssssssssssssssssssssssssssssss ssssssssssssssssssssssssssssssssssssssssssssss ssssssssssssssssssssssssssssssssssss*ssssssssss*

TTTTTTTTT tttttttttttttttttttttttttttttttttttttttt tttttttttttttttttttttttttttttttttttttttttt ttttttttttttttttttttttttttttttttttt*tttttttttttttt*

UU uuuuuuuuuuuuuuuuuuuuuuuuuuuuuuuuuuuuu uuuuuuuuuuuuuuuuuuuuuuuuuuuuuuuuuu*nnnnnnnnnnnnnnnnnn*

V vvvvvvvvvvvvvvvvvvvvvvvvv

WWWWWWW wwwwwwwwwwwwwwwwwwwwwwwwwwwwwwwwwwww

xxxxxxxxx

yyyyyyyyyyyyyyyyyyyyyyyyyyyyyyyyyyyyyyyyyyyyyyy

Z zzzzz

.................................................... ------- -- --- -- - ((((())))) &

1111111 222 33 44 555 66 88 000000

"„"" „ „"„"",,,,,,,,, :: .,,,,,,,,,,,,,,,,,,,,,,,,,,,,,,,

Ursus Wehrli was born in 1969, is left-handed, a lateral thinker and trained typographer. For the last 16 years he and Nadja Sieger have been touring Switzerland, Germany, Britain and New York as the successful comedy duo *Ursus & Nadeschkin*, and have won several awards in this capacity, including the *New York Fringe Comedy Award*. Ursus Wehrli lives in Zurich and works as a comedian, cabaret artiste and freelance artist.

# LIST OF ILLUSTRATIONS